CHURCH CHUCKLES
two

CHURCH
CHUCKLES
two

James A. Weekley

C.S.S. Publishing Co., Inc.
Lima, Ohio

Second Printing 1991

Library of Congress Cataloging-in-Publication Data

Weekley, James, 1938-
Church Chuckles. Volume 2.

1. Christianity — Humor. I. Title.
PN6162.W435   1988   818'.5402   88-6375
ISBN 1-55675-076-4

8873 / ISBN 1-55673-076-4   PRINTED IN U.S.A.

This volume is dedicated in memory of
P. "De" DeArmon Hunter, Jr.

He gave us himself because he was in love
with a deeper "presence."

He cornered the market on spontaneity.

He infused hope with new octane power.

He helped us, his vast congregation-in-
ministry, "to mount up with wings of eagles,
to run, and not give out of gas."

He gave us joy.

Au plaisir.

Grace is a God-grin

When biblical religion became too proper, God would invariably clear the air. He would hit his receivers on the numbers no less. He answered with humor. We see Sarah giggling herself pink when she eavesdrops on an angel's surprise announcement (Gen. 17:21). Jeremiah foretells a new dance — probably called the "Jerusalem Jingle." (31:4) (I wonder if God would have objected if Noah water-skied from the rear of the Ark? Didn't he have the last laugh on Noah when he positioned the rainbow as an upside down grin?) Then there was Jesus. Remember his chemical experiment at the Cana wedding gala? That must have left the *Israel National Observer* buzzing for weeks.

Grace is a *God-grin.* The Bottler of the New Wine smiles down (or from wherever) approvingly on our condition more than we give him credit. If love is the face of God, then grace must come across as his ear-to-ear smile. Joy becomes our gut response to that love. It's a dynamic, contagious tonic. More than tickling our "faith innerds," our joy massages the heart, perks circulation, and gives our organs a "Thanks, I needed that" lift.

Joy's brightest feature flashes across in its directive power. It's a shaker and a mover. Joy acknowledges love's acceptance. That boosts self-esteem. If the meek inherit the earth, then those with a sense of humor give it hope. This book seeks that objective. When humor reminds us that God is caringly on our side (and everybody else's), we take a giant step closer to the millennium of the lion and the lamb.

— Jim Weekley

Table of Contents

"Sour godliness is the devil's religion."

— John Wesley

"Puritanism is the haunting fear that someone, somewhere, may be happy."

— H. L. Mencken

1

Alphas and Omegas

The Old Testament

We begin with a tour of the Old Testament. Before we launch into the "ribbings" of Adam and Eve, we observe the following about creation and the God-complex:

> *Psychiatrist:* "I'm not aware of your problem, so perhaps you should start at the beginning."
> *Patient:* "All right. In the beginning I created the heavens and the earth . . ."
>
> — *Southern Wings*

At our church camp for youth, nestled in the beautiful Blue Ridge Mountains of North Carolina, we have a song about Adam and Eve. Near the end of the verse where the first couple have made their exit, we hear these words:

> "The next day it began to rain;
> And before you knew it, they were rainin' Cain."

Here are some other samplers:

> *Question:* "What time of day was Adam born?"
> *Answer:* "A little before Eve."

"Eve was the first person who ate herself out of house and home."

> — Joe Creason in Louisville
> *Courier Journal*

"Who was the first man?" the teacher asked her class.
"George Washington," a boy answered.
"No, it was Adam," she explained.
"Well, sure," the boy said, "If you want to count
   foreigners."

A Sunday church school teacher asked a girl who the first man was.

"Hoss," she answered.

"Sorry," she said. "It was Adam."

"Shucks! I knew it was one of those Cartwrights."

A child was told by his teacher how Eve was created from the rib of Adam. Later that evening, he complained to his mother, "Mom, my side hurts. I think I'm having a wife!"

— Nancy Browning, Newport, Kentucky.

There is a philosophical twist on this topic. When Adam and Eve were leaving the Garden, he placed his arm around her waist, and with comforting words, said, "My dear, you must understand that we are living in an age of transition."

Noah and Clan

Coming in a close second behind the Genesis One project are the stories circulated about Noah and his cruise ship. We begin with the animals:

Question: "What animal came with the most luggage?"

Answer: The elephant took his trunk."

(The rooster, with his comb, and the fox, with his brush, brought the least.)

The first mention of money in the Bible came when the dove brought the green back to the ark. Noah, of course, ran a tight ship. He allowed no gambling as he sat on the deck. You can bet there was money aboard. The duck had his bill, the frog his green back, and the skunk his scent.

Question: "How can we be certain Noah had a pig aboard?"
Answer: "Because he had Ham."

A Sunday church school teacher was questioning her pupils about Noah. A boy asked, "I wonder if they did a lot of fishing?" "Heck no!" another answered. "They couldn't do much fishing with only two worms."

Question: "Who was the first electrician?"
Answer: "Noah, because he made the Ark *light* on Mount Ararat."

Betwixt Noah and Moses, these stories filter down. A Sunday church school teacher plays trivial pursuit with her students.

Question: "Where is tennis mentioned in the Bible?"
Answer: "When Joseph served in Pharoah's court."

Question: "What do you think 'The Land flowing with milk and honey' will be like?"
Answer: "Sticky!"

Question: "What was the tower of Babel?"
Answer: "Where Solomon kept his wives."

The Sunday church school teacher was describing how Lot's wife looked back and turned into a pillar of salt. One of the students interrupted: "My mother looked back once while she was driving, and she turned into a telephone pole!"

Norma Doblitt

While teaching a class of four-year-olds, the teacher read the story about the twelve sons of Jacob. As she reviewed the pictures, they named the ones they could remember. "Joseph, Dan, Reuben . . ." Then one little girl said, "Blue Jeans." She explained to her teacher that "Blue Jeans" was "Levi!"

Moses

Actors and actresses recite tongue-twisters before going on stage. The late Laurence Newmann, a Yale professor and an authority on semantics, offers this one:

"Moses supposes his toeses are roses, but Moses supposes erronously. For Moses he knowes his toeses aren't roses, as Moses supposes his toeses to be." (I think I'll stick with "Sister Susie's sewing shirts for soldiers.)

The great pontoon project, the crossing of the Red (Reed?) Sea, evoked this response:

A Sunday church school teacher asked, "Who led the children of Israel out of Egypt?" He pointed to one of the boys, who responded, "It wasn't me. We just moved here from Tulsa."

— Mrs. D. Z. Nenstiel, Pampa, Texas

A Mr. Charles W. Moses was the featured speaker at a recent Laity Day observance at the Broad-United Methodist Church in Orlando, Florida. The choral anthem was, "Go down Moses!" Mr. Moses got the message, assuring the choir that by 12:00 noon "I shall let your people go!"

The Ten Commandments give us a humor remedy in "tablet" form.

One boy asked his father, "Did Moses have indigestion like Grandpa?" "Why, son, do you ask such a question?" "Grandpa takes pills for indigestion," he replied, "And the Bible says that God gave Moses two tablets."

Question: Why was Moses the most wicked man who ever lived?
Answer: Because he broke the Ten Commandments all at once.

A woman was mailing the old family Bible to her brother in a distant city. The postal clerk examined the package carefully and inquired if it contained anything breakable. "Nothing but the Ten Commandments," was the reply.

— K. B. Rollins

A sales manager invited his wife and a friend to his son's bar mitzvah. They arrived after the service had started and were seated beside a man who sensed they were visitors. When the rabbi began reading, the old man showed the visitor the proper place for the reading. "These are the laws of Moses," he whispered. "You know — Charlton Heston."

— Earl A. Nielson

"I wonder what the Ten Commandments would look like if Moses had had to run them through a hostile legislature."

(Gov. Ronald Reagan on "The David Frost Show," WBC)

Moses' successor, Joshua, has been exposed as well to the sharp eye of humor.

The greatest miracle of the Bible occured when Joshua told his son to stand still and he obeyed him.

A North Carolina backwoodsman was arraigned with several others for illicit distilling. The court asked his name. "Joshua," was the reply. "Are you the man who made the sun stand still?" Quickly, he answered, "No, sir, I am the man who made the moonshine."

A pastor in a small church dropped in on a Sunday church school class and began asking questions: "Who knocked down the walls of Jericho?" "It sure wasn't me," answered one of the boys. The teacher commented. "Now, Reverend, Timmy's a good boy and doesn't tell lies. If he said he didn't do it, I believe him." Thoroughly upset, the pastor took the matter to the church's board of deacons. After due consideration the board sent the following message to the minister: "We see no point in making an issue of this incident. The board will pay for the damages to the wall and charge it off to vandalism."

— Good News

Here comes the Judge(s):

Question: "Who defeated the Philistines?"
Answer: (from a Sunday church school student): "If they don't play the Mets, I don't keep track of them."

"Samson was the original press agent — he took two columns and brought down the house."

("Observer" in *Financial Times*, London)

On solemn occasions the twenty-third Psalm is recited as a source of comfort. You would never know it in the words of our children.

Miss Murphy, a Sunday church school teacher, was teaching her class the twenty-third psalm. As they were reciting it, she detected that one of the voices was not reciting correctly. She found that one of the boys was saying, "Surely good Miss Murphy shall follow me all the days of my life."

" . . . He maketh me to lie down in green pastures —
and I breaketh out in poison ivy."

— Jack Rose

A child was misbehaving at dinner and his parents
cautioned him to behave. "If you misbehave again,
you'll eat alone in the kitchen," they warned. Sure
enough, he ate in the kitchen. He bowed his head and
prayed, "Lord, I thank you for preparing a table before
me in the presence of mine enemies. Amen."

From Psalm 81:10 was extracted this interesting exegesis:

A man had just opened his dental practice. His mother
decided to embroider a Bible verse to hang on the wall
of his waiting room. The verse chosen was, ". . . open
thy mouth wide, and I will fill it."

— Mary Rose Jensen, Mobile, Alabama

Here is a question about the Psalmist's son:

"What was your Sunday church school lesson
about?" Dad asked his youngster. The daughter replied, "It was about a man named Solomon."
"And what did you learn about Solomon?"
"The teacher said he had 300 wives and 700 cucum-
ber vines."

— Medical Society Bulletin

Play this one by ear:

Question: When did Ruth treat Boaz badly?

Answer: "When she pulled his ears and trod on his corn.

Those forecasters of doom and gloom, the prophets, also have elicited mild reactions.

A student asked his professor following a lecture on the Book of Jonah, "Do you really believe he was swallowed?" His answer: "I tell you what. When I get to Heaven I'll ask him." "But what if he isn't there?" the student inquired. The professor replied, "Well, then you ask him."

Question: Who was Jonah's tutor?
Answer: The fish that brought him up.

Question: When was an automobile first mentioned in the Bible?
Answer: When Elijah went up on high.

There was a mother who regularly quizzed her children on the Bible as they did their household chores. One evening, after a long hard day, she shouted, "All right, who left the light on in the den?" Her youngest child replied, "Daniel!"

— Mrs. Fred W. Clute, Anderson, Indiana

The telephone rang in the newspaper office late one Sunday evening. "Is this the church editor?" "Yes," came the reply. "Well this is Rev. Jones. Do you have the notes from my sermon?" "Yes," the voice said again. "Will you make a correction?

Take Daniel out of the fiery furnace and put him in the lion's Den."

— J. Mildred Myers, Camby, Indiana

"Did you know that Job spoke when he was a very small child?"
"Where does it say that?"
"It said, 'Job cursed the day he was born.' "

"Job wasn't *really* tested — he never had to contend with a stuck zipper."

(Carey Williams, quoted by Leo Aikman
in the *Atlanta Constitution*)

The New Testament

As an open-minded and warm personality, Jesus would have enjoyed the children's reinterpretation of his sayings. Consider these samplers.

A Sunday church school teacher had prepared a lesson on the Sermon on the Mount for her eight-year-olds. She began by asking, "Where do you find the Beatitudes?" Finally, one little girl answered helpfully, "Have you looked in the Yellow Pages?"

— L. O. McDowell, Florence, Alabama

Another Sunday church school teacher asked one of her children to recite a favorite Bible verse. An eight-year-old gave his: "Go ye into all the world and spread the gossip."

— Mrs. L. E. Armour, Pleasant Hill, Louisiana

A Methodist family transferred to a Presbyterian church. The youngest boy continued to pray the Lord's Prayer in the Methodist fashion: "forgive us our trespasses . . ." Finally, his older brother interrupted. "You don't even know how to pray. You're not supposed to say, 'Forgive us our trespasses.' You say, 'Forgive us our debts as we forgive those who are dead against us!' "

Following a teacher's reading of the story of the Prodigal Son to her class of eight-year-olds, a boy asked, "What does it mean to 'waste your substance on riotous living'?" Before she could answer, another boy raised his hand and answered, "It means to spend all your money on bubble gum."

In another classroom discussion of the Prodigal Son, the teacher asked, "When the son returned home, there was one who was not happy, one to whom the feast meant bitterness. Can any of you tell me who that was?" A sad little voice suggested, "The Fatted Calf?"

If the United States adopts the metric system of weights and measurements, that would mean many of our old sayings would have to be updated. Example:

"Let him who is without sin cast the first 6.35 kilograms."

Question: "Who is the smallest man in the Scriptures?"

Answer: "Most of us would say Zacchaeus. Others might suggest Nehemiah (Knee-high-a-miah). Was it not Peter, the disciple who's "slept on his watch"?

"Folks," said the minister, "How many in this congregation have read the 29th chapter of Matthew?" Nearly every hand was raised. Said the minister, "You are the folks I want to preach to. There is no 29th chapter of Matthew! The subject of my sermon this evening is 'Liars.' "

— Mrs. Henry Johnson, Greensburg, Kentucky

There is a church secretary whose phone number differs by only one digit from that of a local bank. She receives many wrong numbers. One day, she answered the phone with these words, "Good afternoon, Christ Lutheran Church." On the other end someone replied, "How about that! I called the money changers and got the temple."

— Joan Soebbing in *The Lutheran*

Lee Tuttle tells the story about a minster preaching on the topic of "The wise and foolish virgins." He began by saying, "The five wise virgins represent the people of light, while the five foolish virgins represent the people of darkness. Now, young gentlemen, the choice is yours. Had you rather be with the wise virgins in the light, or the foolish virgins in the dark?"

There was a wife who refused to travel in airplanes. her husband tried to comfort her with the words of

Jesus, "I am with you always." "Aha!", she replied, "he said, Lo, I am with you always.' "

— A. P.

Well, Almost in the Bible . . .

A woman asked a young boy, "What's your cat's name?"

"Ben Hur," he answered.

"That's a funny name for a cat. How did you happen to pick it?"

"Well," replied the boy, "At first, we just called him Ben. Then he had kittens."

—Bulletin, Jacksonville, Florida

Another little boy was asked to give Paul's definition of God's Word. He remembered that it was something sharp and guessed, "The Axe of the Apostles."

Dr. Marcus Bach was speaking in a church in Iowa. The congregation consisted of farmers and he wanted to get their attention by reading the Scripture as follows: "I am the alfalfa and the Omega." (Now that's food for thought!)

Bible Baseball

In the big inning
Eve stole first; Adam stole second.
Rebecca went to the well with the pitcher;
Ruth excelled in the field;
David struck out Goliath;

Noah gave out rain checks, and
The Prodigal Son made one home run.

2
Minding the Sacred Store

Preaching

Preaching is unique. It's the only enterprise where God tries to pipe his truth through the plumbing of us lesser mortals. Charles H. Spurgeon gave this advice:

"When you speak of heaven, let your face light up and be irradiated with reflected glory. And when you speak of hell . . . well, then your every-day face will do."

_____

A preacher was introduced in this unusual way by one of his laypersons, who prayed:

"Thank you for our preacher today. Fill him with good stuff and nudge him when he's said enough."

_____

The Sermon

The jury is still out seeking a verdict concerning the proper length of a sermon. Some infer that the mind cannot absorb any more than the seat can. My son, Mark, used to slide a hand across his neck . . . closing time. A woman frequently waved a bulletin (not to cool hot flashes).

_____

One Sunday morning a minister apologized to his congregation for the bandage on his face. "I was thinking about my sermon while shaving, and cut my face," he explained. Afterwards, he found a note in the collection plate: "Next time, why not think about your shaving — and cut your sermon."

_____

A few moments before the minister was to deliver the evening sermon, an usher handed him a note. He announced that someone had left their car locked with the lights on. He said, "The implication seems to be that the battery may run down before I do."

— Thomas LaMance, Modesto, California

A minister sold a mule and explained that he was trained to go when the rider said "Praise the Lord;" and to stop when the rider said "Amen." The new owner mounted up and said, "Praise the Lord," and off he raced. The mule was approaching the edge of a cliff and the rider said, "Amen." He stopped. Looking over the edge and wiping his brow, he said gratefully, "Praise the Lord!"

— Sunshine Magazine

A college Bible teacher was concluding one of his lectures by demonstrating the evils of Demon Rum. "I have two glasses of whiskey here on the table; one is filled with water and the other with whiskey. I will now place an angle worm in the glass of water. See how it lives and vibrates with the very spark of life. Now I will place a worm in the glass of whiskey. See how it curls up, writhes in agony, and then dies. Now young men, what moral do you get from this story?" Came an answer: "If you drink whiskey, you'll never get worms."

A minister asked his wife, "Do you know how many outstanding preachers there are in the country today?" She replied, "No, I don't; but I know there is one less than you think."

— *Pulpit Digest*, May, 1972

A preacher was asked to substitute for the regular minister. The speaker began explaining the meaning of a substitute. "If you break a window, and place a piece of cardboard there, that's a subtitute." Following the sermon, a woman shook hands with him, and meaning to make a compliment said, "You were no substitute . . . you were a real pane!"

"Johnny, it's time to go to church."

"But I don't want to . . . the hymns are too old, the sermon is boring, and the people aren't friendly."

"But Johnny, you're 46 years old and you're the preacher."

A difficult church had recently concluded a revival. The minister told a friend, "We've just had the greatest revival our church has experienced in years."

"That's great," replied the friend. "How many members did you receive into the church?"

"We didn't add any but we got rid of three."

A parishioner dozed off in church each Sunday, hoping not to be noticed by the preacher. On leaving church one Sunday morning he remarked, "That was one fine sermon." "I know," said the pastor, "I saw you nodding."

— Mrs. Everett Steven, Sexton, Iowa

An admiring female member of the congregation greeted the minister at the end of the service, saying, "Reverend, I come to these services only because of your fine sermons. They're so wonderful they ought to be published in a book."

"Oh, I don't know," said the minister. "I'm not sure my sermons deserve that much attention. But perhaps they'll be published post-humously."

"That's wonderful!" replied the woman. "I hope I get to read them real soon."

— Mrs. E. A. Stowell, Juneau, Wisconsin

A minister was about to deliver his first sermon. As he expounded, he drank from a pitcher of water until it was almost gone. After the service someone asked one of the elderly members, "How do you like your new pastor?" "Fine," she said, "but he's the first windmill I ever saw that was run by water."

A minister once remarked to his congregation that every blade of grass was a sermon. A few weeks later when he was cutting his lawn, a member passed by and shouted, "That's the stuff, Reverend, cut 'em short!"

— Mrs. Vivian Powell, Jacksonville, Illinois

An active member of a small rural church greeted the minister with this comment after each Sunday's sermon, "That certainly was a good message. They sure did need it." One snowy morning, when no one but the lady showed up for services, the minister, seizing the opportunity, said, "Mrs. Perkins, sit down. I'm going to deliver my sermon to you." He preached on the sin of pride. When he had finished she stood up and said,

"If they'd been here, they sure would have gotten it!"

— Mrs. Elmer Stowell, Juneau, Wisconsin

A priest was trying to get the congregation to participate more in singing hymns during Mass. "Think of it this way," he said from the pulpit, "for those of you whom God blessed with good singing voices, this is your chance to thank him. And for those of you whom the Good Lord did not bless with good voices, this is your chance to get even!"

— John R. Tintle, Buena Park, California

Following the morning service, a minister returned home discouraged over a sermon he had delivered. It dealt with the rich helping the poor. "Well, asked his wife, "did you convince them?" "I was half-successful," he said. "I convinced the poor."

Following a long, dry sermon, the minister announced that he wished to meet with the church board. A stranger appeared at the meeting." "You misunderstood my announcement. This is a meeting of the board." "I know," said the man. "But if there is anyone here more bored than I am, I'd like to meet him."

When a minister died in a rural parish, the congregation called upon the senior deacon to take charge. As he filled the pulpit on the first Sunday, he asked, "How many of you have brought a pencil?" Hands went up. "And some paper?" Envelopes, bulletins, and cards were waved. "Good! We are going to have a contest. Today I want you to write down every mistake I make this morning. Don't hold anything back. The more critical the better. By the way, I'll need to have you sign your name, and the lists will be collected at the conclusion of the worship hour."

It is reported that during the 1880s, the Archbishop of Canterbury gave this advice to his ministers:

"In making a sermon, think up a good beginning; then think up a good ending; then bring these two as close together as you can."

One Sunday I was given an apple pie by one of my Sunday church school teachers. She said, "Now Jim, it's sitting (if pies can in fact sit) on the table in the nursery."

The following Sunday she walked into her room and found the mold-covered pie still "sitting" on the table. She said to me, "Oh my God, you forgot it!"

Even though we became the best of friends, she never baked me another pie.

Preacher and Family

Purchasing some last-minute groceries, a minister found he was ten cents short. "Can you charge a dime?" he asked.

"Forget it," said the grocer. "I'll come to your church some time and take it out by hearing you preach."

"I don't have any ten cent sermons," the minister said.

"That's all right, I'll come twice."

— Rev. W. J. Briggs, Kokomo, Indiana

The new parsonage family was given a pie baked by one who was an average cook. The pie was inedible, so the minister's wife tossed it into the disposal. The following Sunday the minister was faced with the problem of thanking the lady for the pie — while at the same time being honest. When he saw her he said, "Thank you for being so kind and so thoughtful. I can assure you that a pie like yours never lasts long at our house!"

She responded, "Good. Now I want to invite you and your family to Sunday dinner today when you can try three others I baked!"

A minister was pulled over for doing 65 in a 45 speed zone. He said apologetically, "Officer, you wouldn't give me a ticket, would you? I'm a messenger of the Lord." The officer responded, "Well, I'm a messenger of the Lord, too, and I was sent here to save your life." He got the ticket.

In a similar situation a minister was eager to get home after several days absence. He, too, was caught putting the pedal to the metal too far. When pulled over by the officer, he identified himself as a member of the clergy. "Oh, a minister. How would you like for me to preach you a little sermon?" "Skip the sermon," said the minister. "Just take up the collection."

— A. J. Bradley-Low

An associate priest, an avid football fan, had to hear confessions one Saturday during a Nebraska-Missouri game. He asked one of the custodians, "Are you going to be around the church for a while?"

"Yes, Father, I'll be here all afternoon."

"Would you mind, then, reporting to me occasionally on the game's progress?"

"Sure," the man said. Later he made the following report to the confession box: "Father, my last confession was fifteen minutes ago. Since then I ain't done nothing, and neither has Nebraska."

— Jerome A. Langan, *Catholic Digest*

A minister happened to be aboard an airplane ready to crash into the ocean. Everyone was in a high state of panic. Someone said to the minister, "Quick, do something religious." He did. He took up an offering.

The chairman of the board of deacons was informed that his pastor was leaving for another pulpit. "You have nothing to fear," assured the pastor, "I am going to recommend a successor who will probably be a better preacher than I."

"That's what worries me; your predecessor said the same thing."

One Monday morning a minister was surprised to find his wife with her hand in the coins from the collection plate.

"Martha! What are you doing?"

"What do you think I'm doing? I'm looking for a button to sew on your coat!"

— B. T. Jonason, Chicago, Illinois

A minister's wife went to the doctor for a shot. The son asked why she went. The minister said, "To get innoculated." The next day the phone rang and the boy answered. The call was for the mother and the boy said, "She can't come because she's in bed intoxicated."

A burglar entered a minister's modest home at night and woke him. Drawing his knife, the burglar said, "If you yell for help, you're a dead man. I'm looking for money." "Let me turn on the light," said the minister. "I'll help you hunt."

A minister accepted a call to serve a parish in northern Minnesota. The local water supply did not agree with his digestive tract unless a filter were installed in the parsonage water system. The matter was brought before the church board and the secretary reported its action to the congregation the following Sunday: "Moved, and seconded and carried that the trustees take care of the pastor's drinking problem."

— Rev. H. V. Buchholz, Warren, Minnesota

A rural pastor got up every morning and drove to the railway station. There he would watch the train speed through. He commented on the practice: "The train is the only thing that moves in this town that I don't have to push."

— The United Church Observer

The sons of a minister, a lawyer, and a doctor were talking about their fathers' income. The lawyer's son said, "With one case in court, my father makes 2000 dollars." Next, the doctor's son said, "When my father performs surgery, he can earn as much as 3000 dollars." The minister's son, determined not to be outshown, said, "I can top that. For talking just twenty minutes on Sunday morning, my father makes so much money that it takes four men to carry it out."

A young couple, fresh out of seminary, moved into their first parsonage. They were given an old fashioned housewarming. They received many food and clothing items. The most unusual was a container with the following attached note, "Dinner for two. Place in freezer and open only when you are too tired to cook." Months passed and such a day did arrive. They gratefully removed the package from the freezer and opened it. They found a twenty dollar bill with another note, "Redeemable at the restaurant of your choice. Have a pleasant evening."

— Kathleen Hadfield

For Bishops and Other Sinners

Bishops are human and they, too, can get scissored in difficult situations.

The story is told about the late Bishop Ernest Waldorf. He had chaired an all-day meeting in Chicago and headed toward the dining hall. Everything was protocol except for the fact that he couldn't get his bow tie tied. He approached a stranger and asked, "Excuse me, but will you do me the favor of helping with my tie?" The stranger took him to a sofa in the lobby and had him to lie on his back. Quickly, the tie was knotted.

"That's a great job," the bishop said as he looked into a mirror. "But why did you have me to lie down?"

"Well," said the man, "you see, I'm an undertaker."

Like most bishops, the Methodist bishop Jesse T. Peck loved to eat. He was invited to a home for dinner. At bedtime his hostess brought out a pie. It was delicious and he ate several pieces. He retired to bed but began groaning. "Bishop," cried the hostess from another room, "are you afraid to die?" "Nooooo," was the answer. "I'm not afraid. Under these circumstances, I'm ashamed to die."

— Ellen E. Peck, Watertown, New York

First lady: "This is a wonderful meal, bishop. But you don't seem to be your jovial self."

Bishop: "Well, madam, when I came here I was in the best of spirits. Now, all of a sudden, I have taken on a serious illness."

First lady: "That's disturbing, bishop."

Bishop: "I'm fearful that I'm suffering from a paralysis, a numbness over the entire lower half of my body."

First Lady: "You don't mean it!"

Bishop: "I am afraid that is true. All during supper I've been pinching my right leg, and I can't feel any sensation whatsoever."

Second lady: "Oh, if that's all, I can releive your anxiety, bishop. It's my leg you've been pinching!"

A bishop spotted a reporter taking notes on his speech. Later, he asked the reporter to use everything except the jokes. He wanted to use them again while speaking to other churches in the area. The next day, the following line was found in the article: "The bishop told some good stories which cannot be repeated."

— Guston Browning, Henderson, Texas

Some years ago *The North Carolina Christian Advocate* featured this story. A typographical error (the omission of the letter "d") in a church bulletin caused some consternation. There appeared this line item in its annual financial report to the congregation: "The Bishop's Fun . . . $105." Following the meeting, one layman stood up and said, "Why should we pay for the bishop's fun? If the bishop want's to have some fun, he should pay for it himself."

A Methodist Bishop was once asked to name the two most influential books on his life. Without hesitation he said, "My father's pocketbook and my mother's cookbook!"

A noted astronomer was seated next to a bishop on an airplane flight. The astronomer said, "I never had much interest in theology. My religion can be summed up in "Do unto others as you would have them to do unto you." The bishop answered, "I'm fond of astronomy. My views are summed up in "Twinkle, twinkle, little star."

— Lois Maw Cuhel

Roman Catholic Bishop Fulton Sheen once addressed a gathering in Providence, Rhode Island. In his closing remarks he wished the people well. Someone said, "Bishop, I can do anything you can do." He replied, "No you can't, I can kiss your wife but you can't kiss mine."

On How Not to Introduce a Bishop

A minister was introducing his bishop to a large audience. He began with these words: "I know our bishop is pleased to be here speaking in this large auditorium." To make an impression on the bishop, the minister wished to display his knowledge of Latin. He said, "I presume you know the meaning of the Latin word for 'auditorium.' It comes from two Latin words meaning 'audio' (to hear) and tarus (the bull). Now, I wish to introduce . . ."

Methodist Superintendents

A district superintendent was speaking at a church when, midway through the sermon, the lights went out. Through the darkness the minister assured the congregation, "Please, now, we are *de-lighted* to have our D. S. with us today."

— Mrs. Nancy Wingard, Pensocola, Florida

Off to Conference

My friend, Rev. Robbie Moore, Jr., gives us an "Annual Conference Survival Kit." He says, "There are some things almost everyone needs at Conference. These are some that I've come up with, gleaned from years of experience:

    1) *A bottle of No-Doz.* Need I explain?

    2) *A tube of Ben-Gay.* This is for night rubbing of the knee joints. Stuart Auditorium was made for short people. There's no space between the rows of seats, and you have to sit there going through all kinds of contortions trying to get comfortable.

    3) *A Sony Walkman.* It works well during sermons by bishops (they think you're taping them.)

    4) *Handicap sign for your car.* Parking is impossible unless you have one of these signs; . . . you can park right next to the Bishop and the Conference

Secretary.

5) *Bifocals*. You need these to talk to someone closeup while looking around for your District Superintendent — so you can make sure that he sees and knows you're not off playing golf."

The man who opened the conference one year prayed, "Dear Lord, please be with our first speaker and give him power to inspire this group. And be with the second speaker and fill him with your Spirit. And Lord, have mercy on the last speaker."

My first superintendent, Rev. A. Glenn Lackey, shares this story on the reading of pastoral appointments. There was a minister who said after each minister's name was assigned, "God is good." Then, his appointment was read. He was being sent to a six-church circuit. He prayed, "Good God!"

Political Conferences

A couple was touring our nation's capital and the guide called their attention to the congressional chaplain. She asked, "Does he pray for the Senate or the House?" he answered, "Actually, he stands up, looks at the congress, and prays for the country."

The Laity

Church laity see religion more from a practical, everyday slant than from a theological one. Generally, they're more concerned with keeping the local youth group active than with attending Sunday afternoon district meetings (particularly during football season). They, too, can get caught between a rock and a hard place.

There is an actual town in Norway called Hell. It attracts many tourists because of its unusual name. When two Lutherans visited the town, they were quick to send a postcard to their minister in the States. It read, "We passed through Hell today, and we're concerned. Almost everyone here seems to be Lutheran."

—Robert H. Brague, Marietta, Georgia

[Note from the (Lutheran) editor: There is also a Hell, Michigan, a majority of whose residents are non-Lutheran, and who will sell you bumper stickers so that you can announce to other motorists where you have been and back.]

————————————

There was a man who could not remember names. He asked a visitor who had been attending their church for several weeks, "Don't tell me. Do you spell your name with an 'i' or an 'e'? He replied, "With an 'i'. My name is Hill."

————————————

A minister was asked how many of his members were active. He replied, "They all are! Some are active for the Lord and the rest are active for the devil!"

————————————

In a sellout Southern Methodist-Notre Dame football game, a young priest was cheering for the Methodists. During the next time-out a man sitting beside him said, "Father, I can't understand why you're pulling for SMU. Surely you realize Notre Dame is a Catholic insititution!" The priest answered, "First, suh, Ah am a Texan!"

— S. J. Gudge, Tornonto, Ontario

————————————

Some Methodist trustees in a rural church decided to paint the building's exterior. Their budget was limited and they decided they could do the job if they bought only half as much paint as required. They figured they could add an equal amount of water. They did. The following Sunday, it began to rain. It washed off all the paint. As they were leaving the church, a voice from heaven said, "Repaint and thin no more!"

A minister was invited to the home of an elderly woman. He asked why she would not transfer her membership to the local congregation. "I am a Methodist but my membership is back in Georgia." The minister responded, "I'll be happy to write for your church letter." "Well, not now. I am just visiting my daughter." "How long have you been visiting her?" he asked. "Thiry-five years," she said proudly.

— Beverly H. Tucker, Spartanburg, South Carolina

There was a woman who disagreed with everything her minister did. His sermons were either too short or too long. He was either too "chummy" or too aloof. The minister decided to call on the woman at her home. As he approached the walkway, he saw from the corner of his eye that she was peeking out the window. He knocked on the door but there was no answer. Finally, he kneeled down and looked through the keyhole. He saw that she was doing the same thing from the other end. The minister smiled and said, "Mrs. MacDuff, this is the first time we've ever seen eye to eye on anything!"

———————————

"Deacon Jones, I heard you were at the ball game Sunday when you should have been at church," the minister reprimanded. "That's an outright lie," he replied, "and I've got the fish to prove it."

———————————

There was a grandmother who had the good habit of praying the first thing every morning. In her later years she lapsed into reading the newspaper first. One of her grandchildren inquired if prayer had become less important to her. "Oh, no," she responded, "I'm just looking to see what I should pray about."

— Bruce C. Johnson

———————————

Heaven

"My interest is in the future — because I'm going to spend the rest of my life there."

— Charles F. Kettering

———————————

A family was traveling in the mountains. The clouds hung low near the car. The father pulled over to the side of the road near a ledge. The youngest child asked, "Mommy, can we see God from up here?" The mother answered, "No, but if Daddy drives any closer out on this ledge, we will"

— Mrs. Jack C. Graham, Wichita, Kansas

———————————

In his last will and testament, a merchant gave these instructions to his lawyer, "Give the equity I have in my car to my son — he will have to go to work to keep up the payments. My equipment you can give to the junk man — he has had his eye on it for several years. I want six of my creditors for pallbearers — they have carried me so long they might as well finish the job."

There was a long line of men standing in front of the pearly gates, waiting to get in. A sign overhead read, "FOR MEN WHO HAVE BEEN DOMINATED ALL THEIR LIVES BY THEIR WIVES." One man was standing under it. Saint Peter came over to him and said, "What are you standing over here for?" He answered, "I don't know. My wife told me to do it."

— Berl Williams in *Parade*

Little Willie said, "Mamma, don't men ever go to heaven?" "Of course, they do! What makes you ask?" His mother asked. "Because I never saw any angels with whiskers." The mother replied again, "Oh, that's because most men who go to heaven get there by a close shave!"

— Andrew Christian Braun

The devil went to the entrance of the Pearly Gates and tore them down. Saint Peter said, "I'm going to sue you!" The devil responded, "But where are you going to get a lawyer?"

A minister asked a group of children in Sunday church school if they wanted to go to heaven. He was surprised when a boy shook his head no. "Why not?" asked the minister. "Because when this class is over my mother told me to come straight home!"

A Baptist minister went to heaven and was informed by Saint Peter that he would have a Volkswagon for his use. He was pleased until he saw a priest driving in a Cadillac. When he complained to Saint Peter, he was reminded that the priest had to give up having a wife and a family while on earth. He understood. Shortly, he saw a rabbi driving a Rolls-Royce. Again, he complained to Saint Peter. "I can accept the priest's excuse but what can be said about the rabbi? He *did* have a wife and children." "That's true," said Saint Peter. "But remember — he's a relative of the boss."

— Prof. Pierson Parker,
General Theological Seminary, New York, New York

A woman said to her husband, "Be an angel and let me drive." He did and she is. [*Do not be afraid to reverse the sexes in this story.*]

Bargain Basement?

A minister was describing Judgment Day to his congregation. "Thunder will roar; flames will shoot from the heavens; floods, storms, and earthquakes will devastate the world." A young boy turned and whispered to his mother, "When that happens, will I get out of school?"

The devil: "What are you laughing at?"
A junior associate: "I just locked a woman in a room full of hats with no mirror."

There were two ministers who lived in the same town and who had identical names. Naturally, each would occasionally be mistaken for the other. One of the ministers died while the other was attending a summer conference in Florida. The minister at the conference sent a postcard to his wife, but it arrived at the home of the other minister's widow. It read, "Miss you. The heat here is awful."

———————

A young boy had heard the story of the rich man and Lazarus. One day he was counting his pennies and his mother said, "Johnny, you should save those pennies." he replied, "Not me! Do you think I want to get rich and go to hell?"

———————

Following a sermon on Judgment Day, in which the preacher emphasized there will be wailing and gnashing of teeth, a little old lady said to her minister, "Preacher, I haven't got any teeth." "Madam, " he replied, "teeth will be provided!"

— *Butter Spreader*, Reedsburg, Wisconsin

———————

A choir director was explaining some new music to his choir. "Now tenors, I want you to take it to the gates of hell and the rest of you come on in."

— Mrs. John Guthrey, Moravia, Iowa

———————

Famous Last Words (Epitaphs)

There was hypocondriac who died at age 97. His tombstone read, "I *told* you I was sick."

Another tombstone read, "Died at 30. Buried at 60."

Gravestones That Might Have Been:

"This is just my lot."
(Fredrick March)

"Here in nature's arms I nestle,
    Free at last from Georgie Jessel."
(Eddie Cantor)

"Pardon me for not getting up."
(Ernest Hemingway)

From Those Who Died Suddenly

"Died suddenly, nothing serious."

"Went to bed feeling well but woke up dead."

"Primary cause: Blow on head with an ax;
Contributory cause: Another man's wife."

3

Getting the Bees out of Our Haloes

Courtship

Someone defined marriage as an institution that turns a night owl into a homing pigeon. Before the wedding, however, dating must come off smoothly and like clock work. Putting the best foot forward — and not backwards — can "up" our popularity rating. Mark Twain shares this experience:

> One time he called on a woman but got to the livery stable too late. All that was left to pull his horse and buggy was an old homely nag. He arrived at her house later than expected. She was, of course, upset. She decided to make him wait for about a half hour. When she was ready, she opened the door, saw the horse, and said, "Is that the best you can do?" Mark Twain looked at the horse and looked astounded. "I can't believe it! When I got here that was a spry young colt!"

The Wedding

In Doug Marlette's syndicated cartoon strip, *Kudsu,* the minister is asking the couple the traditional questions, "Do you . . . for richer or poorer . . . in sickness and in health" — but adds this footnote, "To have and to hold . . . through Bill's male midlife crisis and Sally having to find herself?"

In the same way another minister asked the couple, "Bill, do you promise to help Mae around the house two days a week?" He replied, "Yes, if she'll mow the lawn every other week!" Sample these other slices from the wedding cake.

> *Dear Abby:* Our son married in January. Five months later his wife had a ten-pound baby girl. They said the baby was premature. Tell me, can a baby this big be that early?
>
> — Wondering

Dear Wondering: The baby was on time, the wedding was late. Forget it.

— Abigail Van Buren

At a wedding rehearsal, the father of the bride appeared the most nervous. In an effort to put him at ease, the minister gave him two simple options and told him to pick one: either, "I do" or "Her mother and I do." The next day as the father escorted his daughter to the altar, he appeared cool and calm. When the minister asked, "Who gives this woman to this man?" he answered, "Her mother and her father and I do."

— Mrs. John Bills, Billings, Montana

A psychiatrist said that "the reason mothers cry at weddings is that their daughters tend to marry men like their fathers."

OOPS . . .

A young minister had been advised that in the event he should forget the marriage vows in the ceremony, he should quote Scripture. As luck would have it, at his first marriage his memory failed him. The first verse that came to mind was, "Father, forgive them, for they know not what they do."

— Mrs. George C. Lucas, Topeka, Kansas

Another young minister got a little nervous in his first ceremony. The ritual read at the conclusion, "It is customary to kiss the bride." He said, "It is kisstomary to cuss the bride."

— Mrs. Frances N. Thomas, Hagérstown, Maryland

Marriage

Once the wedding is history, the couple can get on with the business of living. The right kind of love certainly keeps a marriage glued. A college student from L.S.U. gave this answer when asked on a questionnaire, "Do you believe in college marriages?" "Yes, if the colleges really love each other."

— Lynne Hicks

A minister visited one of his parish families unexpectedly. After knocking on the door, a voice responded, "Is that you, angel?" "No," he answered, "but I'm from the same department."

There was a man who worked on the waterfront. Every day at lunch he would unwrap a sandwich with a bite missing. When asked the reason for the missing section, he responded, "That's my wife's way of saying, "I love you."

"One of the best ways for a wife to surprise her husband on their anniversary is to mention it."

— *Advertiser and News*, Dawson County, Georgia

Mothers

Mothers are almost perfect but thank God they're human. We have to choose our words carefully when philosophising about them. In Methodist circles Susanna Wesley is highly revered for her parenting wisdom. She had nineteen children, of whom only eleven survived infancy.

One morning a Sunday church school teacher asked a student, "What kind of mother did John Wesley have?" Reply: "Nervous!"

Mrs. Ethel Wipp, Escanaba, Michigan

As a highway patrolman was leaving a restaurant, a friend commented, "I suppose everyone gets a ticket today."

"I don't really give out many tickets", he said.

His friends teased, "Now come on, you'd give your own mother a ticket."

"No, my mother never drove a car. But I did catch her jaywalking once. I issued her a warning, that's all."

— D. S. Jones

A mother of twelve was asked how she could take care of all those children. "Well," she replied, "When I only had one it took all my time . . . so how could eleven more make a difference?"

Now, let's observe motherhood from a child's perspective:

"My mother used the ketchup-bottle method: When all else failed, she slapped us on the bottom."

— V. Peter Ferrara

A college student wrote to her grandmother in the hospital, "Dear grandmother," she wrote, "Mother told me you were in the hospital for tests. I hope you get an 'A'."

— Dot Krimm

A New York court awarded a woman $40,000 in damages for the loss of a leg. Other parts of the body are valued as follows:

Arms, at $40,000 . . . . $80,000
Nose $15,000
Eyes at $10,00 . . . . $20,000
Broken heart $250,000

Wives

Like Mom, wives need wisdom too. One wife — who was also a mother — prayed, "Dear God, please give me patience — *and I need it right now!*"

A minister's wife sang in the choir. One Sunday a father asked his daughter if she knew who the wife of the minister was. "Oh, yes," she said, "She's one of the chorus girls."

— Mrs. R. A. Bruehl, Blue Island, Illinois

A wife gave her husband two ties for his birthday. He wore one of them the next day. She said to him, "The other one not good enough for you?"

Fathers

Fathers are important, too. Without them, where would little girls be?

The following announcement appeared in a small town newspaper, "On Wednesday evening, the Ladies Aid of First Church will hold a rummage sale. This will be a good chance for you to get rid of anything not worth keeping but too good to throw away. Bring your husband along."

— Mrs. Imogene Simons, Cherokee, Iowa

The small daughter of a minister watched her father prepare his Sunday sermon. "Daddy, does God tell you what to say?" she asked. "Of course, honey," he answered smilingly; "Why do you ask?" "I was wondering why you scratch out so much."

— Danny Thomas, quoted by Robert W. Pelton,
in *Modern Maturity*

The wife of a naval officer handed her minister a note before he was to deliver his sermon. It read, "John Burkett having gone to sea, his wife wishes the congregation would pray for his safety." Hastily, the minister read it and it came out as follows, "John Burkett, having gone to see his wife, wishes the congregation would pray for his safety."

A father and his son were thumbing through the family photo album. They ran across wedding pictures. The son asked, "Was that the day Mom came to work for us?"

Two men were talking. "My son asked me what I did during the Sexual Revolution," said one, "and I told him I was captured early and spent the duration doing the dishes."

— Orben's Current Comedy

A husband said to his wife, "I know the baby is crying but please remember that 'the hand that rocks the cradle is the hand that rules the world.' " The wife answered, "How about taking over the world for a few hours while I go shopping."

Children go through several stages. First, they call you "Da Da." Then they call you "Daddy." Then they call you collect."

— Los Angeles Times Syndicate

Children

Children do say the "darndest things" about the adult world. When it comes to religion, well, their commentaries are served up as plump wisdom (with a touch of peppermint).

The point has been made that today's parents should have two families, one to raise and experiment with; the other to enjoy.

"The secret of dealing successfully with a child is not to be its parent."

"Before I got married, I had six theories about bringing up children; now I have six children and no theories."

— Lord Rochester

"Insanity is hereditary; you get it from your children."

— Sam Levenson

Here are some kid's questions and comments which have baffled Sunday church school teachers and parents alike.

"When do we get report cards?"

"What if Goliath had been wearing a crash helmet?"

"How can I be thankful if I don't like spinach?"

"How can we get to heaven if we don't get our wings 'til we get there?"

"Why do we look down to pray if God is up there?"

"Who does God pray to?"

"I bet we would have more people come if church were in Disneyworld."

"Dad, can I give a whole dollar like you do?"

"Is the ten-percent tip the same as we give at church, Mom?"

"I heard that same sermon on the radio last night."

A four-year-old girl, on attending the worship service for the first time, was asked, "How did you like it?" "Oh, it was all right, but I didn't think it was fair that the man up front did all the work and then somebody else came around and took all the money."

— Mrs. Charles Woehrer, Valley Farms, Arizona

Equally interesting are their observations on the Sunday service.

"The music was nice but the commercial was too long."

One Sunday morning a little girl said to her mother, "I can't wait to go to Sunday school to see Jesus again!"

"Who does Jesus look like?" the mother asked.

"Well, she has white hair, wears glasses, and a pretty dress with colored flowers!"

The minister met a little boy going into church. He said, "I'm glad you enjoy Sunday church school. Tell me, what do you expect to learn today?" He replied, "The date of the Sunday school picnic."

— Mrs. L. C. Trow, Decatur, Illinois

Recovering from surgery, a minister had mixed feelings when he received a collection of get-well cards from the Sunday church school class. One had these words written: "Please get well soon. May you rest in peace."

After hearing his father preach a series of doctrinal sermons — Justification, sanctification, and other "-ations," he was asked by his Sunday church school teacher, "What does 'procrastination' mean?" His reply: "I'm not sure, but I know our church believes in it."

During a Sunday Mass a priest told about a conversation he had with a little girl. When asked if she believed in God, she answered, "Yes, I do." "Well, why do you believe in God?" the priest asked. "I don't know why. I think it runs in the family."

— Contributed by John E. Dulmage

God definitely has a sense of humor when children address him.

One child, informed by his mother that he might go on a picnic she had earlier opposed, said, "It's too late, Mom. I've already prayed for rain."

"Mom, Billy keeps recycling the first part of his prayers."

A child, moving to another city, prayed, "Good-bye, dear Lord, we're moving to New York. It's been nice knowing you. Amen."

— Karen Bell, Sutter, California

Another little girl concluded her petition with these lines: "Dear God, please take care of Daddy, and Mommy, and my baby sister. And please take care of yourself, or else we're all sunk!"

"Dear God, I am sorry I was late for Sunday school but I couldn't find my underwear."

Eric Marshall and Stuart Hample,
Children's Letter to God

A Sunday church school teacher was instructing her class on the meaning of prayer. She was getting nowhere. She then gave this clue: "What does your father say just before supper?" One girl said, "Take it easy on the butter, kids."

A little girl, almost asleep, prayed these words following here sister's prayer: "Dear God, my prayer's the same as hers."

In a children's message with his children on Sunday morning, the minister encouraged the children to kneel beside their bed and pray nightly. One boy said, "If I did that, it would really be a miracle. I sleep on the top bunk."

A five year old boy was concerned because he had only one prayer which he prayed again and again nightly. His mother suggested he find some prayer books and come up with newer versions. As he left the library, he said, "Gee, won't God be surprised tonight!"

— Mrs. Allen H. Peoples, Santa Monica, California

A little boy was caught with his hand in the cookie jar. His father said, "Son, don't you know God saw you take those cookies?" He said, "Yes, but he didn't see me eat them. I ate them under the table."

A five-year-old boy wanted a brother and asked his father what could be done. His father told him to pray for two months and he'd be given one. At the end of that time, he became impatient and quit. A month later his father took him to the hospital where his mother sat with twins in her arms. The father said, "Now aren't you glad you prayed so much?" The boy said, "Yes, Dad, and aren't you glad I stopped when I did?"

There are other interesting situations where children leave their mark.

A little boy was selling greeting cards to raise money for his congregation's building fund. At one house a lady asked, "Are you selling cards alone?" "No ma'am" he said, "God is working with me, and besides Jimmy is working the other side of the street."

— Mrs. J. Russell Henderson, *Arkansas Methodist*

Art Linkletter once asked a child on his show which came first — the chicken or the egg? "The chicken," he replied, "God can't lay eggs."

A minister from California tells the story about a little girl and the death of her pet kitten. To console her, her mother said, "Don't worry, honey, your little kitty has gone to heaven to be with God." With a tear in her eye, the little girl said softly, "But what would God do with a dead cat?"

Every Sunday morning a woman brought her six children to church on time and a bit rumpled. Another mother of only one child asked her how she managed to get them all ready? "Easy," she said, "I dress them the night before!"

Mary F. Martin, Jackson, Mississippi

A little girl was asked, "What is the capitol of Hawaii?" Without batting an eye, she answered, "Hallelujah!"

It has been said that the greatest miracle of the Bible took place when Joshua told his son to stand still — and he obeyed!

Lee Tuttle shares the story about a business manager who wanted to challenge human nature. When his daughter came in to work one morning she found a penny, a quarter, a fifty-cent piece, and a twenty dollar bill on her desk. Shortly, he came into the office and asked her, "Which one would you like to have?" She said, "My mother always told me to take the smallest piece, so I will take the penny, but if you don't mind, I will take this piece of paper here to wrap it in!" She picked up the penny, wrapped it in the twenty dollar bill, and left.

A minister, while making a pastoral visit in a home, asked if he could read a chapter from the Bible. The father asked his son to go get "the big book we read so much." He did. He returned with a mail-order catalogue!"

— Margaret Faith, Camden, New Jersey

A father became irritated when his small son scratched away on his violin. A dog howled nearby. Finally, the father said impatiently, "Son, can't you play something the dog doesn't know?"

A four-year-old girl called her mother. "Mommy, my goldfish died." The mother tried to comfort her. "Honey, I know this is a hard time for you. I'll be home shortly and we can talk about it." "But Mommy, I have to ask you a question now." The mother replied again, "Go ahead, dear. Ask your question." "Mommy, would it be all right if we eat him for supper?"

Contributed by Betty L. Hagerty

My former bishop, Gerald Kennedy, tells about one of his preaching experiences. He got started on schedule and the congregation was responsive. Then a baby began crying "somewhere between joy and anguish." The mother and father smiled bravely, oblivious to his squalling. The bishop pressed on. Shortly, a child dropped a hymnal and cried for a drink of water. Near the end of the sermon the baby took the hiccups. The bishop said, "Brethren, did you ever try to conclude between hiccups?"

Finally, from the secular side, we note these:

A small girl was asked, "What are you going to do when you grow up big like your mother?"
Her answer: "Diet!"

Youth

"Adolescence is a period of rapid change. Between the ages of twelve and seventeen, for example, a parent ages as much as twenty years."

Changing Times, The Kiplinger Magazine

A father and a son were working together on a traveling wheat harvest crew in Kansas. The father began instructing the lad on the precautions about the machinery. "Be careful of the belts and chains on the combine. Remember, one hand on the wheel and one for steadying yourself. God gave you only two hands." Again, the father said, "Be careful of your feet. Don't let them get hung in the auger or gear. God gave you only two feet." Finally, he instructed, "Wear safety goggles. God gave you only two eyes." The son had the last word, however. "Yes, and thank God he gave me only two parents."

— Contributed by Pat Fredrickson

One youth confessed, "When I was twelve I was almost converted by a church movie until the projector broke down."

Around the House

A youth said to his father, "It's time I became more independent! It's time I was treated like a man! It's time I stood on my own two feet! But I don't see how I can do it on my present allowance!"

A wife cautioned her husband, "Bill, you had better help Johnny with his homework today, while you can. Remember, he enters the fifth grade this fall!"

Top Agers

Our senior citizens' group has a nickname. XYZ'ers means "Extra Youth and Zest." Having a name like that is like having an after-burner. Our club is very much alive! Here are a few observations on arriving there . . .

Middle Age: "When actions creak louder than words.

— Dana Robbins, quoted by Red O'Donnell in
Nashville *Banner*

Advice to people over forty: "Keep an open mind and a closed refrigerator."

— *Nuggets*

Old(er) age occurs when there is silver in the hair, gold in the teeth, lead in the pants, and iron in the veins.

"Aging is mind-over-matter. If you don't mind, it doesn't matter."

— Quoted on WCBM-Radio, Baltimore

You are getting old when your back goes out more often than you do.

There are four signs of old age. "The first is loss of memory; the second is . . . I forgot the other three."

"I can live with my arthritis.
My dentures fit me fine.
I can see with my bifocals.
But I sure do miss my mind."

On purchasing a new pair of glasses, a lady from Mississippi observed, "I was driving fine until I got my glasses. Now cars are coming from every direction."

There are three ages. (1) Young; (2) Middle; (3) "My, but you're looking good."

"If I'd known I was going to live so long I'd have taken better care of myself."
— Casey Stengel

Satchel's Rules for Staying Young:
"1. Avoid fried meats, which angry up the blood.
  2. If your stomach disputes you, lie down and pacify it with cool thoughts.
  3. Go very light on the vices such as carrying on in society. The social rumble ain't restful.
  4. Don't look back; something might be gaining on you."

"I'm still here. I've had a very exciting life, and I expect the second half to be even better."
— George Burns

These comments were heard in church:

Every Sunday an older couple hold hands during the worship service. When complimented about their love and dedication, the wife responded, "Love has nothing to do with it. I hold Harold's hand to keep him from cracking his knuckles."
— Contributed by Birdie L. Etchison

A minister reminded an older member that he should be giving some considerable thought to "the hereafter." The man suggested that it crosses his mind several times a day. "That's very wise," he said. Finally, the man said that it was not a matter of wisdom. "It's when I open a drawer or a closet and ask myself, "What am I here after?"

— Quoted by Eric W. Johnson in *Older and Wiser* (Walker)

Several elderly church members were being asked what it was to which they attributed their longevity. When one wealthy lady was asked, "Why has God permitted you to live to the age of ninety-two?" she responded, "To test the patience of my relatives."

A little girl was visited by her grandmother. That evening before going to bed, she prayed, "Dear God, Don't forget grandmother. Please bless her and let her live to be very, very old. Amen."

In Passing . . .

An excited wife exclaimed to her friend, "I've cured my husband of biting his nails!" Her friend asked, "After all these years, how did you do it?" She replied, "I hide his teeth."

— Lee Tully

On their 50th wedding anniversary, a couple spent the day receiving well-wishes and gifts from friends and relatives. In the evening the honored couple were resting in the den. The husband said to his wife, "Martha, I'm proud of you!" "What's that, Pa?" she said. "You know I can't hear without my hearing aid." Speaking louder, he said, "I'm proud of you!" "That's all right," she murmured. "I'm tired of you, too."

A grandmother had just arrived at her grandchildren's house. Her grandson said, "I'm sure glad to see you. Now maybe Daddy will do the trick he's been promising us." "What's that?" the grandmother asked. "I heard him tell mommy that he would climb the walls if you came to visit us."

A physician said to his patient, "The pain in your right leg may be due to old age." "Impossible," replied the patient. The other one is the same age and its all right."

An excited wife exclaimed to her friend, "I've cured my husband of biting his nails!" Her friend asked, "After all these years, how did you do it?" She replied, "I hide his teeth."

— Lee Tully

On their 50th wedding anniversary, a couple spent the day receiving well-wishes and gifts from friends and relatives. In the evening the honored couple were resting in the den. The husband said to his wife, "Martha, I'm proud of you!" "What's that, Pa?" she said. "You know I can't hear without my hearing aid." Speaking louder, he said, "I'm proud of you!" "That's all right," she murmured. "I'm tired of you, too."

A grandmother had just arrived at her grandchildren's house. Her grandson said, "I'm sure glad to see you. Now maybe Daddy will do the trick he's been promising us." "What's that?" the grandmother asked. "I heard him tell mommy that he would climb the walls if you came to visit us."

A physician said to his patient, "The pain in your right leg may be due to old age." "Impossible," replied the patient. The other one is the same age and its all right."

4

Purple Dragons and Other (Nearly) Divine Goodies

Ecumenical

Paul Harvey, the radio newsman, tells of an incident involving Methodists parking in the Baptist parking lot on Sunday mornings. It became a delicate situation and the Baptist congregation didn't want to offend members of the neighboring congregation. So they decided to place bumper stickers on all cars in the parking lot. They read, "I'm proud to be a Baptist!" It solved the problem.

A Hindu, a [*fill in your denomination; we'll refer to it here as "Brand-X Christian"*], and a Jew were driving to an ecumenical conference. The car broke down and they had to spend the night at a farmer's house. There was only one bed and one had to sleep in the barn. The Hindu volunteered to sleep in the barn. Later that night, there was a knock on the door. The Hindu said, "I can't sleep out there because there are cows in the barn. They are sacred and we can't do that." The Jew said he would go to the barn and sleep. Shortly, there was another knock on the door. The Jew returned and said, "I can't sleep out there, either. It's just not kosher to sleep with pigs." The Brand-X Christian said he would sleep in the barn. Again, in no time, there was another knock at the door. When they opened it, the pig and the cow stood there.

Easter

Trying to explain the Resurrection to children isn't always easy. One teacher attempted by employing the analogy of a butterfly emerging from a cocoon. At death, she explained, our souls, like butterflies, are released from our bodies. Then, we wing our way toward God where we will live with him forever. One child observed, "But I saw a dead butterfly yesterday."

A church planned an Easter pageant. On the night of the dress rehearsal, Pontius Pilate had to work. A member of the choir substituted. As they began rehearsing Pilate's solo, the conductor of the orchestra said, "Pilate, I don't hear you. You're not loud enough." The substitute said, "Pilate is at work. I'm the co-Pilate tonight."

— Bill Dyson, Fairburn, Georgia

A youth said, "I'm giving up spinach for Lent." Another promised, "I'm giving up woolens for lint."

A church organist overslept on Easter morning. The Sunrise Service was scheduled for 6:30 a.m. At 6:31 the minister called to see if she was on her way. She had just gotten out of bed. The following year, early on Easter morning the minister remembered the incident and made sure the organist was on time. At 5:45 a.m. the minister called and said, "Christ is risen, and you'd better be too."

— Cathy Norman, Elyria, Ohio

Halloween

It's quite a jump from Easter to Halloween. The smile of God, however, is not confined exlusively to sacred days.

Today, many churches observe All Saints' Day by asking interested members to dress in costumes depicting a saint or a biblical character (or event). One boy came to such a party dressed in a football uniform. When asked what the significance of the uniform was, he replied, "You mean you've never heard of the New Orleans Saints?"

— Tulsa World

One Halloween night the telephone rang. The mother picked up the phone and these words were heard: "Trick or treat!" Then the operator said, "Your treat is a call from your daughter. The trick is, she's calling collect. Will you accept the charges?"

— John I. Beavers, Tooele, Utah

Q: What did the mother spook say to the baby spook?
A: "Don't spook until you're spooken to."

Thanksgiving

A maid who served in an English mansion was instructed to address a royal family with "Your grace." As they came through the front door, she welcomed them with these words: "For what we are about to receive, we are truly thankful. Amen."

A college student returned home just in time for Thanksgiving dinner. She was astounded to find a lavishly prepared dinner. Even more remarkable was the fact that her mother was not one of the best cooks in the family. The matter was cleared up, however, when her father offered this prayer: "Our Father, we thank you for this fine day. We thank you for our fine daughter. Most of all, we thank you for Harry's Delicatessen, which made this dinner possible."

— Contributed by Michael Walker

A mother hen, experiencing difficulty in making her chicks behave, said, "If your father would see you now, he'd turn over in his gravy."

— Helen Daley in *Capper's Weekly*

Franklin D. Roosevelt once told a gathering about a priest who had been robbed. Following the theft, the priest entered these lines into his diary: "Let me be thankful. — *first,* because I have never been robbed before; *second,* because he took only my purse, and not my life; *third,* because although he took all I had, he did not take much; and *fourth*, because it was he who stole, and not I!"

Christmas

A child asked her mother, "Does Santa Claus bring us presents?"
"Yes," replied the mother.
"Does the stork bring us babies?"
"Yes," the mother said.
"Does the police department protect us?"
"Yes," the mother said a third time.
"Then, what do we need Daddy for?"

But we all need Christmas. Usually, the first week of December you begin feeling it in the air. One church made this proposal on its front bulletin board: "Stop here for your holiday Spirits."

— Pat Loftis

One little boy was excited over his part in the congregation's Christmas play. "What part did you get?" asked his father. "I'm one of the three wise guys," he replied.

An eight-year-old boy had a part in the Christmas play. His parents were so excited that they bought him a new jacket. In the play the boy was to announce the cast of characters as they appeared. To make certain he would not forget his lines, his father pinned them just inside his new jacket. When the time came, the boy announced: "That is Jesus in the manger. Mary is nearby, and Joseph is standing next to her. The three wise men are named . . . er . . . er . . ." He could not remember, so he took a quick peek inside his coat and blurted out, "Hart, Schaffner, and Marx!"

John Thompson

Two sisters were looking at a painting of the Virgin Mary and the Infant Jesus. "But where is the father?" one asked. "Oh, he's taking the picture," the other replied.

— James Dent in Charleston, West Virginia, *Gazette*

The Flight

Following the fanfare at Bethlehem, the Holy Family found it necessary to flee to Egypt. Again, children offer their own flavored exegesis.

One little girl explained the reason his parents took Jesus with them on the flight into Egypt: "They couldn't get a babysitter."

Students in Sunday church school class were asked to draw pictures of the Holy Family. All were conventional — Mary riding on a donkey, and the like — except for one. It was a picture of an airplane with four heads sticking out of the window. The young artist announced proudly, "This is a picture of the flight into Egypt." His teacher said, "And who are the passengers?" The youngster quickly identified Joseph, Mary, and Jesus. The teacher asked, "But who is the fourth?" He answered, "Oh, that's Pontius the pilot!"

A professor was invited to lecture at the University of Cairo. An airplane strike was in progress and it was difficult to get tickets for his wife and himself. Professor Joe, as he was called, finally received confirmation two days before takeoff. An airplane employee sent him this memo: "Flight into Egypt for Joseph and Mary confirmed!"

— Mary V. Michel, San Antonio, Texas

The New Year

A "cool" college student thought he could handle any situation and talk himself out of anything. He didn't do too well on his mid-term exam, and wrote this excuse across the front page, "Only God knows the answers. Merry Christmas!" Later, he got his paper back with this reply, "God gets an A. You get an F. Happy New Year."

— Bob Steele in *Parade*

"We jingle the bells in December and juggle the bills in January."

Oops . . . . . (Bloopers)

To err is human but to commit bloopers . . . well, most of them are overlooked (with the possible exception of a few choice ones like the following).

The following announcement appeared in a Sunday bullentin: "The flowers on the altar will be given to those who are sick after the sermon."

From a bulletin in South Carolina church: "There will be a monthly Deacon's meeting next Sunday morning. It will be gin with breakfast at 7:30 a.m."

This one is unusual but interesting: "The afternoon homecoming will be highlighted with sinning in the choir."

"I shall be away for the next few Sundays. The preacher during my absence you will find pinned to the church notice board, and all births, marriages, and deaths, will be postponed until my return."

Contributed by Roy R. Palmer of
First Unitarian Church, Cincinnati, Ohio

After Dinner

Before addressing an audience, a psychiatrist received this strange message from his wife: K.I.S.S. (translation: Keep It Short, Stanley!)

After a flowery and lengthy introduction, a featured speaker said, "My mother would be grateful and my mother-in-law would be astounded!"

Franklin D. Roosevelt offered the following advice to his son, James, on making a speech: "Be sincere; Be brief; Be seated."

One speaker, having addressed an audience for fifteen minutes, had still said nothing. He said, "After eating such a fine meal, I feel that if I had eaten any more, I would be unable to talk." From the far end of the table came these words, "Give him a sandwich."

One year a church's father-son banquet fell on St. Patrick's Day. A rabbi, who wore a bright green tie, offered the prayer. Before praying, he made this comment: "I've never felt so safe and at peace. The devil would never dream of looking for a Jewish rabbi in a Methodist Church on St. Patrick's Day."

— Contributed by A. G. Addington

Etc.

"The only exercise some church people get is jumping to conclusions, running down their friends, side-stepping responsibility, and pushing their luck."

These lines appeared on a church bulletin board: "Help stop truth decay."

— Tulsa Baptist Church

An artist in Belgium once cleaned the interior of one of the old cathedrals damaged after World War II. His bill:

Embellishing Pontius Pilate and putting a ribbon on his his bonnet $50.20

Putting a tail on the rooster of St. Peter and mending his comb 33.00

Re-pluming the left wing of the guardian angel 41.80

Correcting the Ten Commandments 57.20

Rebordering the robe of Herod and adjusting his wig...41.80

Cleaning the ears and putting shoes on Baalam's ass...30.00

Putting earrings on Sarah's ear 20.40

Putting a stone in David's sling, enlarging the head of Goliath, and extending his legs.............30.20

Decorating Noah's ark 30.00

Mending the shirt of the prodigal son and cleaning his ears 40.00

Improving Heaven, adjusting the stars, and cleaning the moon 51.50

Re-animating the flames of Hell, putting a new tail on the Devil, and mending his left hoof 53.70

Acknowledgements

One score and five years

> I've brought forth these humorous pieces;
> Some came with out names like uncles and nieces.
>
> Others, are tagged by a proper doner.
> (I've done my best to document)
> Scout's honor!
>
> (Also, used on congregations in a flash . . .
> and passed off safely as heavenly hash.
> *Deo Gratias.)*

— Jim Weekley

About the Author

James "Jim" F. Weekley, pastor of Ebenezer United Methodist Church, Belmont, North Carolina, has previously served congregations in California, West Virginia, and Western North Carolina. He is received his Ph. D. degree in philosophy from Pacific Western University. He is currently included in *Who's Who in Religion in America.*

He is married to Rosalyn Creel, an elementary school teacher. They are the parents of two college students, Sharyn and Mark.

He is past chairperson of the Family Life Council of the Western North Carolina Conference. He has been an instructor of logic at Sacred Heart College.

He has authored the following books:

- *Two on a Grapefruit*
- *Marriage is Something Else!*
- *On Bringing Us Together*
- *Making Love a Family Affair*
- *Wings of the Spirit*
- *Recycled Hallelujahs*
- *Beginnings*
- *Praise and Thanksgiving*
- *Tilted Haloes*

He has also contributed to numerous periodicals and journals.